A *Sisterhood* of STRENGTH

DIONY GEORGE

CFI

AN IMPRINT OF CEDAR FORT, INC.

SPRINGVILLE, UTAH

To my beautiful daughters, Krischa and Ambri, with whom I not only have the privilege of being their mother, but also share the Strength of Sisterhood.

ISBN 13: 978-1-4621-1076-6

Published by CFI, an imprint of Cedar Fort, Inc., 2373 W. 700 S., Springville, UT 84663
Distributed by Cedar Fort, Inc., www.cedarfort.com

LIBRARY OF CONGRESS CATALOGING-IN-PUBLICATION DATA

George, Diony, author.
 A sisterhood of strength / Diony George.
  pages cm
 Summary: A collection of stories about women who have served or been served by others.
 ISBN 978-1-4621-1076-6 (alk. paper)
 1. Female friendship--Religious aspects--Christianity. 2. Christian women--Religious life. 3. Christian life--Mormon authors. I. Title.

 BV4647.F7G46 2012
 248.8'43--dc23

                                        2012016333

Cover design by Angela D. Olsen
Cover design © 2012 by Lyle Mortimer
Edited and typeset by Michelle Stoll

Printed in the United States of America

10 9 8 7 6 5 4 3 2 1

Printed on acid-free paper

God Gave Me
A SISTER

When God sent me down to earth,
He knew how hard it would be.
He knew I'd need someone to love and understand me.
So God gave me a sister,
a sister as a friend. A special soul who'd love me and
help me endure to the end.

God knew I would grow weary,
He knew the days would be long. He knew the trials would
come often, He knew I'd have to be strong;
God knew I would have problems,
He knew I'd need a helping hand. He knew I would want
someone
to listen with her heart and understand.

When sisters truly love each other, their spirits often unite
with the added strength of a sister,
it's easier to do what's right. That's why God gave us all sisters,
Sisters as our friends.
Special souls who love us and help us endure to the end.
Oh God, help us to be sisters,
Sisters as well as friends,
Special souls loving and helping others endure to the end.

—Author unknown

Other Books by
DIONY GEORGE

Torn Apart
Imperfectly Beautiful

Acknowledgments

A special thanks goes out to all the wonderful women who made this book possible by sharing their stories, including those who wished to remain anonymous.

Anne Bradshaw*

Afton Graf

Amy Maddocks*

Anita Wahlstrom

Brooke Cosper

Carol Kerr

Cheri Chesley*

Cher Park

Connie Sokol*

Cynthia Robbins Newman

Deanne Blackhurst*

Debra George Hunsaker

Elaine Stinnett

Haley Hatch Freeman*

Heather B. Moore*

Jaime Theler*

·❧· ACKNOWLEDGMENTS ·❦·

Jane Davis

Jodi Robinson*

Kate Nielsen

Linda Kay Garner*

Lori Nawyn*

Merada Gregory

Pam Bolla

Roslyn Reynolds*

Vickey Pankhe Taylor*

Yvette Scott

and others

* published author

Contents

CONTENTS

Preface

THE PHONE CALL

The one calling in the Church I'd dreaded ever being asked to accept was teaching Relief Society. I'm not sure exactly why it scared me so much—I'd held many other teaching callings through the years—but it did.

On a late fall afternoon, I was cooking dinner. The phone rang; it was my husband. He was having car trouble and needed me to come pick him up. I had barely hung up the phone when it rang again. This time it was the bishop. He asked if we could come over to the church and meet with him right away. After explaining I was just on my way out the door, we agreed on a time to meet the next day.

I merged onto the freeway into rush hour traffic and tried to settle in for the thirty-minute drive. I couldn't help wondering what the bishop wanted to talk to me about. I knew the ward Primary president was moving. I inwardly groaned, hoping it had nothing to do with that. I was currently serving as the Relief Society enrichment leader and had been for about six months. I enjoyed it and felt I was finally handling the calling. I didn't want to be changed. What was it then?

In came a quiet impression—I was going to be called as the new Relief Society president. *That's not funny*, I felt like shouting out loud. That was a calling I didn't want to contemplate. It had to be something else.

A rush of fear flooded my body. I became more distraught. I cranked up the volume on the radio—anything to distract myself. For the rest of the drive, I pushed the crazy thought away.

That night after family prayer, my husband and I got ready for bed. I climbed in more than ready to burrow beneath the covers and open the book I'd been reading. In the quiet, my earlier impressions returned. This time, the names of two women in the ward came to me with a feeling they were supposed to be called as my counselors. It wasn't long before a name for a secretary followed.

I had a hard time falling asleep.

By the time my husband and I left the next night to meet with the bishop, I had calmed down a little, but on the way into his office and up to the very moment he extended the call as Relief Society president, I was hoping my impressions had been wrong.

It was amazing how quickly I became much less frightened of teaching Relief Society compared to being called as the new president.

Two weeks later, I taught my first lesson to the sisters in my ward—I survived! I had been worried I might need to run out during the middle of the lesson to throw up. At the end of class one of the sisters came up to me with a big smile on her face and told me what an excellent teacher I was. I'm not sure how I was able to thank her graciously without choking, but there was no doubt in my mind I'd experienced a little miracle that day.

During the time I was privileged to hold that calling, my faith in Heavenly Father grew immeasurably as I learned to more fully rely on Him. He filled my heart with Christlike love for the women in my ward, and a deeper bond of sisterhood strengthened inside as I was blessed to serve them.

I hope as you read and ponder this collection of true and inspiring stories about women—sisters—you will feel that same love and strength in your own life.

—Diony

"Each of us has a vital role, even a sacred mission to perform as a daughter in Zion. . . . It is our time, and it is our destiny to rejoice as we fill the earth with greater kindness and gentleness, greater love and compassion, greater sympathy and empathy than has ever been known before."[1]

—Mary Ellen Smoot

LOVE HAS NO BORDERS

She didn't live in our neighborhood. She wasn't LDS. When she became gravely ill, I wondered who would help her. Our ward was warm and friendly, but would they reach out to someone they didn't know? I wasn't sure. How much could they give?

I visited with Jill (not her real name) in her kitchen along with a neighbor and a volunteer from her church.

"I'm sorry," the volunteer said, "but it's December, you know, and people are busy getting ready for Christmas. I just don't know how much we'll be able to help."

"I didn't choose December," countered Jill. "Why don't you talk to God about it?" Jill's congregation covered a large geographical area, and I knew that was complicating things. Her church members didn't live nearby.

"You know, Jill," I said, "Maybe December is the perfect time to help. I can't think of a better way to celebrate the birth of our Savior. I'll help, and I'll bet my friends will too." I was thinking of my Relief Society sisters. They had generous and tender hearts, but was this too much? I wasn't the Relief Society president. Did I even have a right to ask?

"We'll help too," said Jill's neighbor.

Jill had received contaminated nutritional supplements. They had been manufactured out of the country and marketed here.

Evidence suggested that they were laced with harmful substances. Across the country was a growing handful of suffering people who had taken the supplements before they had been pulled from the shelves.

Class action lawsuits would eventually surface, but for now, Jill had pressing needs. She had a number of serious medical conditions with names I couldn't pronounce. She might die or become permanently disabled. She needed help with basic needs, like food and getting to the bathroom. Her husband had to go to work because bills had to be paid.

Jill's neighbors, her church members, and I agreed that we would split the days we would help. We would bring her lunch, check up by phone, and someone would come twice each day to take her to the bathroom, besides at lunch. I would be asking my Relief Society sisters to do very personal things for someone they had never met. We didn't know how long Jill would need our help. It could be a long time.

I explained the situation to my Relief Society and invited them to give an incredible gift. They did not disappoint. We took every third day, rotating with Jill's other friends. Each week, sign up sheets were passed around and miraculously filled up. I took all the vacant spots, but there weren't many.

Sisters signed up for lunch, dinner, phone checks, and bathroom visits. Soon I heard of sisters who stayed to fold clothes or throw in a batch of laundry. Some loaded or unloaded the dishwasher and others vacuumed. Understanding Jill's loneliness, some stayed to visit.

When the weather warmed up, some sisters did yard work. I arrived with lunch one day to find my neighbor mowing Jill's lawn. Someone suggested that occasionally we gather at lunchtime with potluck and picnic around Jill's bed. My sisters wanted to do more than help out. They cared about her. They wanted her to feel their love.

The weeks stretched into months. I cannot recall how many. On one occasion, we were invited to fast and pray for Jill. Jill's congregation would fast and pray, and so would her kind neighbors.

My Relief Society sisters met together in the stake center to close our fast. Women from other wards joined us. The word had spread. Since I was Jill's friend, I was invited to pray. It was an honor. I marveled at the strength of the sisterhood to which I belonged. I felt God's love for Jill, and I knew that she was His beloved daughter and my sister.

Jill's husband was exhausted. Although we helped with her needs during the day, he cared for her through the night after working a full day. He also took care of her on weekends. Several of my Relief Society sisters volunteered to spend the night, leaving their families and freeing Jill's husband for a night of uninterrupted sleep.

Jill and Monte were reluctant to accept this kind of help. They allowed me a test run. Jill worsened in the night and was hospitalized the following day. I wondered if she was dying. Her body was hardening. Her organs were shutting down.

After a lengthy hospital stay and experimenting with various treatments, Jill returned home stronger and began to recover. She eventually returned to teaching school (with only a few disabilities) and is living a rich life.

I seldom see her, and those sign-up sheets are long forgotten. For a time we shared a miracle, my sisters and I, a miracle of love.

Love is an interesting thing. We love our family and our friends. We love our neighbors, especially those who are agreeable. We love those who love us, and sometimes we love those who are hard to love. I didn't know if we could love strangers, but my Relief Society sisters showed me that we can. They showed me that love has no borders.

—Linda Kay Garner

"A beautiful, modest, gracious woman is creation's masterpiece. When a woman adds to these virtues as guiding stars in her life, righteousness and godliness and an irresistible impulse and desire to make others happy, no one will question if she be classed among those who are the truly great."[2]

—David O. McKay

2

DENISE

My experience of being blessed by visiting teaching wasn't a one-time event, but rather the service was bestowed for months and years. Pregnancy is a trying time for me. Severe morning sickness and extreme fatigue leave me completely bedridden for the entire nine months. I have to be treated with cancer patient medication to keep any food down and to prevent me from losing weight. Dehydration is an added complication.

I was enduring my second pregnancy when a compassionate woman named Denise, from my ward, was assigned to be my visiting teacher. I was interested to find out that, like me, she too experienced great hardship while pregnant. It was rare to find someone who truly understood the physical helplessness. She told me that she wouldn't have survived her own pregnancies if it weren't for service by her own visiting teacher. She promised herself then to pay it forward.

I didn't expect more than a much-appreciated meal, but when she brought me food, she immersed herself in the kitchen to clean, do dishes, and cater to my son's needs and mine.

I was self-conscious and I suppose proud at first about her help, but I realized I was in no position to turn away her service, especially when I prayed daily for relief. The answer to my tearful pleading to my Father in Heaven continually was, "Let others help you."

For months, Denise brought me unexpected meals, always doing dishes and helping where she could while here. I know on a couple of occasions she felt impressed to come. I remember her telling me that she felt she needed to check on me, and in response to the Spirit, she immediately dropped everything to come to my aid.

In February, my beautiful daughter was born and my health returned. Denise was released as my visiting teacher, but our friendship continued even though life kept both of us busy and we rarely were able to spend time together.

Years passed. Then one spring I was surprised to hear that my kind friend was once again assigned to be my visiting teacher. Within a couple weeks, I found out I was pregnant again.

From the moment she knew of my news, she was at my door once again with love and empathy. This time the trial of pregnancy had increased due to my responsibility for two other children's needs.

Denise not only served me as before, but she also came every Tuesday for the entire nine months. Her services extended to cleaning my bathrooms, straightening rooms, caring for my children, and even rubbing my feet and holding me up as she assisted me to my bed at night.

When the cold season hit our family, she brought home remedies and essential oils to nurse us back to health. Whatever our needs were, she saw them and did all she could to bring us relief.

I was touched deeply by her willingness to help me and by the demeanor in which she did it. Denise was always smiling cheerfully, and I often heard her singing or whistling as she did the dishes or swept the floor. I saw love radiating from her—not just love, but Christ's love.

Denise taught me what it means to truly serve the way Christ wants us to and how to completely fulfill our calling as visiting teachers. I will be eternally grateful to Denise for her immense

service to me and my family. I know she will be blessed for her devotion.

I rejoice in knowing that Heavenly Father truly meets our needs through His serving angels, visiting teachers.

—Haley Hatch Freeman

"I feel to invite women everywhere to rise to the great potential within you. I do not ask that you reach beyond your capacity. I hope you will not nag yourselves with thoughts of failure. I hope you will not try to set goals far beyond your capacity to achieve. I hope you will simply do what you can do in the best way you know. If you do so, you will witness miracles come to pass."[3]

—Gordon B. Hinckley

3

He Had Not Forgotten Me

I was going through an especially difficult time in my life. I had recently been divorced and was struggling financially to support myself and my three young sons living in a large city away from extended family. I was experiencing great feelings of loneliness.

I would kneel and pray often, but the feeling just wouldn't leave. I know it was my own pain that prevented me from feeling God's love in my life at this time. I know now that God was there protecting us, but I just couldn't feel it in my great sense of pain and loss.

As I had so little money, it was hard to do anything fun. With careful budgeting to pay my bills, I had just enough to buy gas for the next two weeks with my paycheck, but that didn't include anything extra.

Holidays were terrible for us that year. We didn't have any family to spend them with, and those weekends dragged by. I wished so much that someone would invite us to spend the holidays with their family. That Thanksgiving, I didn't even have the money to put together a Thanksgiving dinner. My birthday was about a week before the holiday, and I just wished I could have a pumpkin pie for my birthday.

One night just before Thanksgiving, there was a knock at the door of my apartment. When I opened the door, two sisters who said they were my visiting teachers stood holding a pumpkin pie. They wouldn't come in, as they said they had to hurry.

I never saw them again, but I felt that pie was the Lord's way of answering my prayers and His way of telling me He had not forgotten me.

—Afton Graf

"Your Heavenly Father knows your name and knows your circumstances. He knows your fears and frustrations, as well as your hopes and dreams. And He knows what you can become through faith in Him."[4]

—Jeffrey R. Holland

4

SISTERS—AN ETERNAL GIFT

I was an only child for over nine years, and every day for as long as I can remember, I prayed for a brother or a sister. When I found out my mother was going to have a baby, I was so excited. I was in fourth grade when my sister was born, and when I went to school that day, I told everyone I possibly could I had a new sister.

When my parents brought her home from the hospital, my mother said that if I got a pillow from the bed and put it on my lap, I could hold her. I sat in the big chair, and my mother gently laid her in my arms. Afton had big brown eyes and dark hair and was so little. I thought she was beautiful, and I loved her instantly.

Three years later, my mother had another baby. My parents named her Elaine. She had blue eyes and blonde hair, and I loved her just as much. I felt so lucky to have two little sisters. I don't remember ever getting upset with them over anything. I had waited for what seemed like forever to have them, and all I wanted to do was protect them, care for them, and help them any way I could.

My sisters have been two of my best friends during my life. We have cried and laughed together, shared our fears and concerns, our heartaches and joys, and our testimonies with unconditional love and support. We've gone through so much, and we're so close I couldn't imagine us not always being there for each other.

In 1992, Afton was diagnosed with breast cancer. I was devastated. How could my life continue without one of my sisters? How could I ever deal with her being gone?

For the next several years, Afton fought her cancer bravely. I was awed by her strength and admired her great faith. Many times when she prayed, I was sure if I opened my eyes I would see Heavenly Father and the Savior standing close by.

She went to several doctors and willingly tried different treatments, hoping to be healed. As the cancer spread throughout her body, I knew this was something I couldn't fix. I couldn't take away her increasing pain or prevent her from growing weaker. So many times I wished I could.

Afton was an example to many. When visitors came to see her, hoping to lift her spirits, they were uplifted by her. She had one visiting teacher that came over almost weekly for months to talk with her and keep her up to date on things.

When Afton passed away, Elaine and I knew she'd been released from her mortal body to return to the presence of heavenly beings who loved her. Our last act of service for Afton—as her sisters—was to dress her for burial. It will be a day of rejoicing when we all are reunited again.

I am so deeply grateful for sisters—my sisters and the many sisters I have touched lives with in the Church. They've taught me so much about life, facing challenges, strengthening my testimony, and, yes, even how to die, as I have served them in their last days of their mortal existence. I've been blessed through the visiting teaching program in Relief Society far more than I have blessed those I visit.

—Merada Gregory

"Cherish one another, watch over one another, comfort
one another and gain instruction that we may all sit
down in heaven together."[5]

—Lucy Mack Smith

5

SHE COULD NOT SEE HER

One night, a sister deep in thought over the Lord's plan for her future felt prompted to go to him in prayer and simply ask. Because the hour was late, her husband and children were long asleep, and their home was peaceful and still.

She was on her knees to begin when a feeling of darkness surrounded her, causing great uneasiness. She had experienced such a thing before and knew the adversary was present. Fear gripped her heart until she remembered Satan only had the "power to bruise her heel" while she, through the power of Jesus Christ, had the power to "crush his head."

She relates, "I began to pray fervently to the Lord that he would send his protective angels to watch and guard over me."

Instantly, the darkness lifted and was replaced with a wonderful feeling of joy and love. In a way not expressible in words, she sensed the presence of her recently departed grandmother.

"So strong was the feeling, that I quickly opened my eyes and turned to where I could feel her presence. I fully expected to see her standing there. Though I could not see her with my physical eyes, I could point to the spot where I knew she was standing. I felt of her comforting spirit the remainder of my prayer."

She learned that night that the Lord can and does use women to strengthen and minister to other women.[6]

—Anonymous

"Each sister, no matter where she stands, can look to either side and feel the spirit of inspiration coming back as she extends the gentle hand of charity to those on either side."[7]

—Boyd K. Packer

6

Applesauce Cupcakes

During a lesson one Sunday in Relief Society, I heard a story about a sister that lived near a woman she didn't really like. She found fault with everything the woman did and labeled her as being stuck-up. She heard the woman thought the same thing about her.

The woman wasn't very friendly, yet when they passed each other, the sister gave her a cool nod or said a polite hello. However, the feelings of dislike she harbored toward this woman were making her unhappy. One day, she heard the woman was ill. At first she thought, *So what?* It wasn't her concern. Then she realized it was. Her conscience got the best of her, and she went to her kitchen and made a batch of applesauce cupcakes.

She took some over to the woman's home. The woman's face lit up with surprise and pleasure. A warm feeling spread inside the sister, erasing all the angry prejudices she'd had. When she walked home, she was smiling, and suddenly the day was much more beautiful and bright.

That woman became one of her dearest friends. Someone once said, "Hate is love gone wrong." We hate those whom we might have loved.[8]

— Cora Hill Arnold

"Let all bitterness, and wrath, and anger, and clamour,
and evil speaking, be put away from you with all
malice: And be ye kind to one another, tenderhearted,
forgiving one another, even as God for Christ's sake
hath forgiven you."

—Ephesians 4:31–32

7

MARCI

*N*ot long ago, I had made a pot of my family's favorite broccoli cheese soup for dinner. It was later than usual, my husband was still at the office, and I'd been running errands. The kids and I gathered around the table to eat, then afterward I sent them upstairs to get ready for bed. I began cleaning up the kitchen. I opened up the dishwasher and quickly glanced around the room to see what dishes, if any, I had missed.

Right then I had an impression. *Bring Marci some of your soup.*

At first, I brushed it off. I reasoned that it was already way past dinnertime, and besides, I knew there wasn't enough soup left to constitute leftovers. Broccoli cheese soup was one thing my family would eat without someone complaining, and they all had eagerly enjoyed seconds. But as I began gathering up a few more plates, something else miraculous happened.

I looked at the refrigerator door.

There written in a black, erasable marker on my whiteboard calendar was the name Marci. And would you believe it was written on that exact day's date? I had written her name on my calendar the previous Sunday as a reminder to set up a visiting teaching appointment. So there I was at seven thirty at night on a Wednesday, unable to deny that this was the day the Lord wanted me to serve my sister.

Marci had been a less-active sister since I had moved into the ward, but she seemed to be taking baby steps to returning to full activity. Again, the prompting beckoned me.

Bring Marci some soup.

I looked inside my oval-shaped CrockPot to assess the soup situation. I doubted there was even enough for a full bowl, but with a rubber spatula I managed to scrape the sides and the bottom of the pot, filling a plastic container with enough soup for a single serving.

Next, I picked up my cell phone and sent Marci a quick text message asking if I could stop by. Within seconds, Marci texted me back.

"Yes, I'm home and I'm feeling a little under the weather and I'm just lying down watching TV. Come by anytime."

You know that feeling you get in your throat just before you start to cry? Well, that started happening. It was such a simple thing—a plastic container full of broccoli cheese soup, and yet, Marci needed it. And a loving Father in Heaven knew it.

Learning to trust those impressions is what make us trusted servants of God. On that night, I knew it wasn't my soup that Marci needed, but my soup was the means by which I could go and minister to a sister in need. It was a way to let her know that I cared.

"How did you know?" Marci responded as I handed her my soup.

"Oh, I just did," I said with a smile.

Bringing soup to Marci was an ordinary task but one that blessed me with an extraordinary testimony of how important it is to listen to those small and seemingly insignificant promptings. For if we do, we learn that it is by small and simple means that great things are brought to pass.

—Jodi Marie Robinson

"Women . . . who can hear the voice of the Lord, and who respond to those promptings, become invaluable instruments in His hands. . . . Never doubt that your influence is absolutely vital to preserving the family and to assisting with the growth and spiritual vitality of the Church."[9]

—M. Russell Ballard

8

LOVE NEEDS NO WORDS

*I*t was the fall of 2004, and my husband and I were making a long-awaited trip to Veracruz, Mexico. I had never been farther than Tijuana, and I was looking forward to this trip with great anticipation. My husband and I had been budgeting money for several months. We'd made child-care arrangements and saved up our vacation time from work.

A few days before we were scheduled to leave, my eighty-eight-year-old grandmother fell in her apartment and fractured her left shoulder. She was rushed to the ER, but the doctor said that the damage was minor and that she should heal quickly. However, he recommended that someone stay with her for a few days to keep an eye on her.

If it had been serious, I wouldn't have gone. My grandmother and I had always been close. But she wouldn't hear of it. Grandma had been almost as excited about my upcoming trip as I'd been. She'd traveled to Mexico several times herself, and she had a great love for the people and their culture. I promised I would tell her all about the trip when I returned a week later.

My husband and I left the Salt Lake City airport Friday morning before the sun rose, and after several plane changes and a three-hour bus ride, we eventually reached our destination of Martinez de la Torre.

Mexico was humid and full of tropical flowers and lush greenery. We breakfasted on fresh mangos and melons and spent Saturday touring well-known Indian ruins. We arranged to attend a small local ward for our meetings at nine in the morning the following day. However, before we could leave, we received a phone call from our oldest daughter. Through her tears, she told us the shocking news. During the night, grandma had passed away in her sleep.

I couldn't believe it. Grandma had been sore from her fall when we'd left, but the doctor said it wasn't serious. She'd been alive only a few hours before. How could she be gone?

I was still in shock as we took a taxi to the gray-brick chapel in the middle of the city and found our seats for sacrament meeting. But as first one and then two hours passed, my emotions thawed, releasing an overwhelming rush of pain and grief. I struggled to control my feelings through Sunday School, holding tightly to my husband's hand, but by the time I reached Relief Society, it was all I could do to keep from bursting into tears.

The sisters in Relief Society spoke no English, and with the grief that was choking my throat I didn't even try to explain about my grandmother's death in Spanish. I felt alone and far from the comfort and consolation I so badly needed.

On my right sat an older woman with gray streaks in her jet-black hair. Her large, chapped hands and thick muscular arms spoke of a life of hard physical labor. She was a stranger whose life and culture were so different from my own.

She looked over at me for a moment when I sat down, before turning her gaze away. Then, a few minutes after the meeting began, she made an unexpected movement. She shifted toward me so that her arm pressed against mine. It was a simple act, but to my surprise the warmth of her skin on mine brought with it an overwhelming sensation of understanding and comfort.

We never spoke to each other, but she stayed close to me throughout the rest of the class, and I felt as if somehow she was sharing my pain while offering me her support and strength in return. Without a single word, she'd been able to communicate all the love and friendship I so desperately needed during that difficult time.

We left for home as soon as the meeting was over, and I never got a chance to thank my new friend. I never learned her name or anything about the life she led. Yet that act of kindness one Sunday morning when my world seemed to be falling apart will remain in my memory and my heart for the rest of my life.

I realized that day that participation in the gospel and our innate feminine gift of empathy creates a powerful bond that connects all women of the Church—a relationship as sisters and daughters of God that transcends language barriers and overcomes cultural differences.

—Deanne Blackhurst

"No matter what circumstances you sisters experience, your influence can be marvelously far-reaching . . . in your example of righteousness and the countless gentle acts of love and kindness done so willingly, so often on a one-to-one basis."[10]

—James E. Faust

9

FEED HIS SHEEP

I recently heard from two sisters I used to visit teach. They appreciated that every month I would copy the visiting teaching message from the *Ensign* page and highlight key points. I either delivered it to them at work or left it on their door with a treat. I never let the fact they were too busy keep me from delivering the message.

One of the sisters was less active and had been for years, but she welcomed me. I tried to be friendly, non-judgmental, and consistent. I moved fifteen months ago, and to my dismay she hasn't had one visit since. My visits for six years were the only link she had with the Church.

I moved out of the ward after several years of visiting teaching one sister, but I still see her every year on Christmas Eve—her husband's birthday. He is not a member. We haven't missed a visit in more years then I can count. Someone called to ask how I had gotten to see this sister. She was having no luck visiting her. I told her I cared about being her friend—first. It was never about just marking a visit off my to-do list.

I don't want to stand in front of my Heavenly Father someday and say I was too busy to check on my sisters. I agreed to be a visiting teacher. We may never know the impact we have on a sister we teach, but I do know our lives and theirs are better if we do as the Lord asks us to do—feed his sheep.

—Brooke Cosper

"The world has enough women who are tough; we need women who are tender. There are enough women who are coarse; we need women who are kind. There are enough women who are rude; we need women who are refined. We have enough women of fame and fortune; we need more women of faith. We have enough greed; we need more goodness. We have enough vanity; we need more virtue. We have enough popularity; we need more purity." [11]

—Margaret D. Nadauld

10

JULIE

O urs was a friendship that, over the years, dissolved into what could be termed as a mere acquaintanceship. I left the neighborhood we both lived in and vowed to return to see Julie as often as I could. She was going to become a real estate agent; regrettably, I don't know if she ever got her license.

Through the grapevine, I heard she moved into an apartment across town. I didn't think of her again until I opened the newspaper one evening. Amid op-ed pieces, wedding announcements, and local news stories, one article caught my eye. It was about Julie's young son.

He'd been injured in an accident and, after several months, lost his battle to live. A little voice told me I should go see my old friend, give my condolences, and try to be of support. It wasn't just the kind of fleeting worry that makes you wonder if you should return home to check and see if the stove is still on—and you do and it's not. It was the kind of voice that shouted, "Go home. The house is going to burn down!"

But time was short, my life busy. I ignored the prompting.

The following Wednesday, the paper came again. That same little voice, as if in a reprimand, instructed me to turn to the obituaries. There she was—Julie—her life over, my chance at keeping my promise to remain her friend snuffed out. I trembled with remorse.

What years ago had brought us together were the differences and similarities that eventually kept us apart. We were both strong-minded women with individual goals we worked hard to attain. However, we had both yearned for a relationship with our Lord and Savior and happiness and stability for our children. In the beginning, I set out to be an example Julie would be proud to emulate, a supposedly solid friend in whom she could trust.

In the end, I was so busy trying to be a good person in the eyes of the world that I forgot the world is composed of individuals. Could I have made a difference if I kept my promise to return and see her? Would it have mattered if I paid my respects when her son died? Put my arms around her, giving her all she once looked to me for? My mind told me I couldn't know for certain, yet my heart whispered the truth.

It can be argued that it is not humanly possible to keep track of all the people who come and go in our lives. But the Spirit will never fail to guide us to where we are truly needed if we will but heed the call.

Yesterday is over, but each new day is a gift. An opportunity to strive to stay in tune with the Spirit; an opportunity to remember other Julies in my life and pray I will never forget them again.

—Lori Nawyn

"Sisters, strengthen yourselves by seeking the source of true strength—the Savior. Come unto him. He loves you. He desires your happiness and exults in your desires for righteousness. There is no burden we need bear alone. His grace compensates for our deficiencies. Your strength will strengthen others—your children, your husband, your friends, and your sisters in the gospel." [12]

—Chieko N. Okazaki

11

NICOLE

Years ago, I put myself through college at Brigham Young University by working on campus and at the Missionary Training Center. Though I diligently worked part time and attended classes full time, often my wages (loosely named) didn't adequately cover my expenses.

I don't remember how hard life really was, but I do remember walking to classes, searching the ground for quarters and dimes (because an apple from the vending machine cost thirty-five cents). Before you shed a tear, know that I also scrounged money for midnight pizza and ice cream (college essentials must be attended to).

At one point, I roomed with three other girls, and we shared a four-shelf cabinet for our food that sat behind the kitchen table. We each "owned" a square shelf. One week, I opened my cupboard and, like the nursery rhyme, found it completely bare. For a moment, I stared at the other three compartments, chock-full of tasty-looking boxes and cans of "food, glorious food." I closed the cabinet door and went to class, wondering what to do.

Later—I'm not sure if it was that day or the next—I remember opening my front door to find Nicole, a girl I barely knew, standing there. She was holding a heavy bag of groceries and smiling. After inviting her inside, I told her of my predicament and how she was an unbelievable, and timely, answer to prayer. We unloaded the groceries and chatted. Although we had only recently met and connected, I realized she was a unique and lovely person. And I came to find out this type of service was not unusual; it was just her way to be aware of others' needs and then fill them.

Today, we're still great friends, and my cupboards are full (without her intervention). In fact, my shelves overflow with cans and boxes—a throwback to my college experience, I suppose. But I can say that over the years, I've tried to emulate Nicole's example. Not because I'm amazingly philanthropic, but because I know exactly how it feels to have nothing in the cupboard, or on the table, with no apparent way to change it. And it simply feels good to be a surprise solution to someone else's empty shelf.

—Connie Sokol

"And behold I tell you these things that ye may learn wisdom; that ye may learn when ye are in the service of your fellow beings ye are only in the service of your God."

—Mosiah 2:17

12

THE CIRCLE OF SISTERHOOD

July 25, 2005

Dear diary,

Today started a whole new chapter in my life.

My doorbell rang. It was my bishop, bringing the jolting news a wife never wants to hear. My husband, Michael, had been killed at the National Scouting Jamboree he and my son had been attending. There had been an accident—Michael was gone. Question after question raced through my mind. What will become of our little family now?

For the next two days, over three hundred visitors flowed through our home—it amazed my children and me. The support we received for the next three months was the most empowering thing I had ever experienced—I knew we would be just fine. As the weeks and months since Michael's death passed, the lives of almost everyone around us returned to normal. The real journey of putting the pieces of our lives back together truly began. One day I realized a constant in my life—eight amazing women, my dearest friends, including my mother, had been by my side. They were always there helping me live normal life—lunches, movies, walks, short get-away trips, wonderful phone calls just to chat—helping me make sense of everything.

One of these women had stayed all night at my house the day Michael was killed, concerned about me being alone until my parents arrived. She sat by my phone day after day, taking hundreds of messages for me. I had a mother and father that dropped their whole life to rescue a daughter with a broken heart. They became my confidants.

Hearts melded together for eternity. They all brought a feeling of normalcy to my life amid the challenges of raising four children alone. How do women—of no relation other than friends—become like sisters? It is the passion and charity women inherently receive as a gift from God.

Our lives had already changed so much; then we were told to move to Utah, a place my children and I had never been, except passing through on the way to somewhere else. I know it was truly divine intervention. Our family was ready. It was a chance to start over. Such a peace came over us and I knew exactly where in Utah to go.

We found a house in Bountiful, two doors down from the temple. I felt safe. The weeks and months began to go by, and once again I realized the constant in my life. Four new, wonderful women had become dear friends, doing the same kinds of things that held me steady before. Nothing huge. Just simple acts of kindness and caring—the endless circle of sisterhood.

—Carol Kerr

"One person can make a difference. Each one of you has unique gifts. Use your gifts to serve others. As we walk in His light, we become women of courage and conviction. We become women of vision, women of destiny, and women of eternal value. We are a worldwide circle of sisters."[13]

—Mary Ellen Smoot

13

"He Loves You"

It had been a stress-filled week, and I was overwhelmed—a familiar feeling since I had begun serving as the Relief Society president in my ward. As a wife and mother of seven, I was already plenty busy, and the added responsibility caused the thoughts and concerns circling inside my brain to run on only one speed—fast forward.

When I finally made it to bed that night, feeling exhausted, I quickly fell asleep. In the early hours of the morning, even though the house was quiet, something woke me up. My eyes were heavy as I looked around the room and then closed them again.

A name of a sister in my ward came clearly to mind. I needed to visit her that day. She had been in my thoughts a couple of times over the past few weeks, but I had pushed them aside. We were good friends, and I felt sure that if something was wrong, she would have told me.

I called her that morning as soon as the kids left for school. She answered right away. I was relieved to find out she was at home. Her voice sounded surprised when I asked if I could come over to see her.

Less than thirty minutes later, I was standing on her porch pricked by a twinge of nervousness—strange. She opened the door promptly and invited me in. We sat across from each other in the living room.

"I wanted to check on you and see how everything's going," I said.

"Everything's fine," she told me with a smile.

I hadn't expected that. *Then why am I here?* I wondered.

"How's your husband doing?" I asked.

"He's good," she said.

I asked her about her children.

Her response was the same. "We're all doing good, thanks." I was puzzled.

"Well . . . you've been on my mind a lot the past few weeks, and this morning when I woke up, I felt I needed to come see you today," I explained.

Her eyes widened to a stare.

I could see she was struggling inside from the emotions crossing her face. I waited. When she was ready, she let out a breath. She and her husband had been trying for quite a while to have another baby.

"I really feel like we are supposed to have one more," she said "I'm not getting any younger. At age thirty-five, the chances of having a baby with Down syndrome go up quite a bit. . . I'm not that far away." Her face was troubled. "I had a miscarriage recently," she wiped at her eyes, "and I've needed to know that the Lord was aware of me . . . aware of my situation, and that he cared."

"He is, I know," I said. I felt inspired to say, "He loves you."

More tears fell and we talked for a few more minutes until I felt I should leave. I gave her a hug, happy to see the light had returned to her eyes. Within several months she was pregnant again. She carried the baby to full term.

—Diony George

"Every calling provides an opportunity to serve and to grow . . . I urge you to see it as an opportunity not only to strengthen and bless others but also to become what Heavenly Father wants you to become."[14]

—Dieter F. Uchtdorf

14

A Choice Sister

I met Charlotte when my husband and I lived in Oklahoma early in our marriage. I was the youngest child and the only girl in our family of five children, so Charlotte became my first experience of the blessings of sisterhood. Her kids were older than mine. Lydia, her youngest, was the same age as Brandon, my oldest—they became fast friends. I came to rely on her for parenting advice, especially after my twins were born.

Jeffrey, one of our twins, had an undiagnosed digestive issue for the first ten months of his life. I became adept at timing his projectile vomiting sessions to minimize the mess, and as a result he never did it at a doctor's appointment. At nine months, an upper GI test showed a blockage just under his stomach. A consultation was scheduled at the children's hospital in Oklahoma City for the next month.

The Monday before the appointment, both twins woke up with the stomach flu. Charlotte came and picked up Brandon while I looked after two sick babies. By 6:00 p.m., Daniel was able to keep down water, but Jeffrey hadn't had a wet a diaper since the night before. Concerned about dehydration, I called some friends to help me get the boys to the hospital.

Daniel was going to be fine in couple of days, but they admitted Jeffrey to the hospital. He needed surgery. What followed was ten stressful days at the hospital, worrying about my baby. My husband, Bryan, left his job in Wyoming and flew back to stay with me and Jeffrey.

I never had to worry about Daniel and Brandon. Charlotte had her hands full with five kids of her own, but she took in my two little boys—even as sick as Daniel was—and cared for them like they were hers. Daniel was put on a special medicine to suppress vomiting so he could keep food down. Charlotte kept me updated regularly by phone. After the first few days, Bryan went home to take care of our boys. But, for a while, it had been all up to Charlotte.

For a long time, I bore the kind of guilt a mother has when two of her children need her but she can only be with one. Daniel had been very, very sick, but I had to be with Jeffrey.

The children's hospital in Oklahoma City was a two-hour drive from our home, and I couldn't go back and forth. I couldn't dream of leaving Jeffrey in the hospital alone. Because of the timing, I missed caring for Daniel through his first serious illness. It helped me greatly to know he was in good hands.

I'd trust Charlotte with my children's lives, and I have. Even though years and distance now separate us, I feel like I could walk into her life at any time—or she into mine—and we'd pick up right where we left off.

—Cheri Chesley

"What greater gift dost thou bestow,
What greater goodness can we know
Than Christ-like friends, whose gentle ways,
Strengthen our faith, enrich our days."[15]

—Karen Lynn Davidson

15

UNEXPECTED FRIENDSHIP

J hardly noticed the sun was shining in the sky that day, even as its bright rays came blindingly through my kitchen window. My marriage was ending. My husband, who had become a stranger, moved out a few days before. I was lonely and discouraged.

My younger children woke up from their naps, and my three-year-old immediately wanted to go outside. His two older brothers were already out, but I wasn't in the mood to listen to complaining if I asked them to watch him.

I changed the baby's diaper and picked him up. My toddler eagerly headed for the door. I reminded him of his boundaries before he hurried off to play. I sat down on the front steps to watch and put the baby on my lap. After several minutes, I stood up to stretch my legs and walked to the end of the driveway to check the mailbox.

Joan lived across the street and had been part of the neighborhood for about as long as my family had. Whenever we saw each other, we'd call out a polite "hello" or "how are you today?" Sometimes we just waved. Her family seemed like perfectly nice people. There wasn't a specific reason we didn't know each other better—we were just busily going about our own lives.

Joan saw me getting the mail and came over, starting the longest conversation we'd ever had up to then by commenting on how much my baby had grown. We talked for a good fifteen minutes until my toddler interrupted. He needed to use the bathroom. I gave Joan a hurried good-bye and took him quickly in the house.

After cleaning up a wet pair of underpants and encouraging my son to keep trying, the baby was hungry. I nursed him, and then it was time to start dinner.

Over the next couple of days, Joan and I talked a lot. She was warm, and I felt more comfortable around her than I expected. We became fast friends—I felt a deep connection to her. I already had incredible support from my extended family and many friends, but Joan started filling an unconscious void I was carrying inside.

She was married, about my age, and had three children. She wasn't a member of the Church, but she was a dedicated Christian, a wife, and a mother who loved the Lord. For the next several weeks, she spent time with me almost every day or we talked on the phone.

Joan's love and unexpected friendship made a big difference in helping me get through that extremely lonely and difficult time of my life. I'm sad to say that when I moved from the area we ended up losing touch.

As I've thought about her over the years with gratitude and fondness, I've come to believe Joan was an "angel-sister" placed in my life by the Lord at the specific time I needed her.

—Diony George

My Sister's Hands

My sister's hands are fair and white; my sister's hands are dark
My sister's hands are touched with age, or by the years unmarked
And often when I pray for strength to live as He commands
The Father sends me sustenance in my sister's hands

My sister's hands are lined and worn with burdens of their own
And yet I know that should I mourn, I need not weep alone
For often as I seek His grace to lighten life's demands
The Father sends me solace borne in my sister's hands . . .[16]

—Becki Madsen

16

A SILENT HUG

J was going through a very difficult separation. Very few people in the ward knew what was going on. However, I had confided in my visiting teachers. Each visit, they brought a message that lifted me, and they listened with compassion to my hopes and dreams that somehow happiness and peace might come to our family once more.

In the midst of that separation, my husband drowned. He was taken to a hospital, and the children and I waited in the hall outside the emergency room for what seemed hours until the doctor emerged to tell us that despite all they had tried, they had been unable to revive my husband. He was gone.

It was late, and we drove home, devastated. I don't think any of us slept much that night. The next morning as I was at the dining room table, making burial arrangements with the funeral director, the doorbell rang, and one of the children answered it. I turned to see one of my visiting teachers coming up the stairs, tears in her eyes. She walked over to me, looked into my eyes with compassion, gave me a big hug, and then turned and hurried out.

Not even a word was spoken, but I knew she loved me and was feeling my pain. Each time I think of that moment, I think of how we covenant to "bear one another's burdens" and how

she did that for me that day. I learned from her that even when I don't know what to say, I can show love, and it can make a difference in someone's life.

—Roslyn Reynolds

"Be not weary in well-doing, for ye are laying the foundation of a great work. And out of small things proceedeth that which is great."

—Doctrine and Covenants 64:33

17

Facebook and the Lord

I was called as Young Women president one year ago. I had not been in the Young Women program, other than sports coach, since I graduated from high school. Needless to say, I was scared. I had a daughter in Young Women, but Heather had only been in for four months and was just as new to the program.

I knew that Personal Progress had changed and that the General Young Women Presidency had added a new value— virtue—the previous summer. I didn't know much more. After being trained, I felt strongly I needed to focus on the new value. I didn't know where to start. What could our presidency do to help the girls learn how to be virtuous young women?

About the same time, I created an account on Facebook. My husband was leery about social networking, but I looked at it as a way of connecting with old friends. One of the first friends I found from high school had recently published a book called *Torn Apart*. I bought a copy and read it.

After finishing it, I decided I needed to contact her and tell her about my new calling. I told her about the challenge I was faced with. I truly felt like the Lord was leading me to where I needed to go.

She told me about another friend, also an LDS author, who had written a book called *Women of Virtue*. I got a copy and devoured the pages and its message. I knew the Lord wanted her to come speak to my Young Women—she had the message they needed to hear.

I can't say that our Young Women are now living the value of virtue perfectly since attending the fireside, but they do know they are daughters of Heavenly Father and what that means.

—Kate Neilsen

"More than ever before we need women of faith, virtue, vision, and charity . . . women who can hear and . . .women who rejoice in their womanhood . . . their identity, their value, and their eternal destiny. [And] above all, we need women who will stand up for truth and righteousness and decry evil at every turn and simply say, 'Lord, here am I, send me.'"[17]

—M. Russell Ballard

18

ANNELIESE AND EVELYN

One morning, while serving as a Relief Society president, I was busy with some projects and left an hour late for my usual morning walk. Whenever I'd reach the busy intersection at the stoplight, I always crossed the street to avoid the traffic.

That day, I didn't—I turned left. In the distance I could see a young woman. When I got closer, I realized it was Anneliese. She had recently moved into the ward, and I had gone to her home to visit her, but she hadn't attended church yet.

Her face was filled with worry. She asked me if I knew where the bus stop was. She needed to get downtown for an important appointment. Unfortunately, the closest one was quite far. I told her that we could return to my home and I would drive her to the appointment. Anneliese made her appointment in plenty of time. I told her how much Heavenly Father loved her and wanted to help her.

How did I know? It was simple—I never walk at that time of the morning, and I never walk down that street. No other sister in the ward would have recognized her because she was new. It was not a coincidence—it was one of Heavenly Father's tender mercies that had placed me in the right place at the right time.

Another time, I was with my husband after he had been assigned to be Evelyn's home teacher. She was in her eighties and lived in a gated community for seniors. After she lost her husband, her physical strength started to decline, and she spent many hours in bed. If she didn't feel up to having visitors, she wouldn't answer her phone or open the gate.

One Sunday evening, we went to visit Evelyn. Another resident opened the gate for us. I called Evelyn while we stood on her doorstep, and her phone rang and rang and rang. There was a light on inside—I was sure she was home.

My husband suggested maybe it was one of the no-visitor days and perhaps we should try again another time. I felt we should check on her. I knew where she hid a spare key because she had difficulty walking to the door. I found it and opened the door.

"Evelyn," I called. There wasn't an answer. I looked around, and called again. Then I saw her—on the floor in the living room. She was propped against a couch cushion with an afghan over her legs.

"Are you all right?" I asked.

She told me she had fallen in the kitchen Saturday evening. Unable to get back on her feet, she had dragged herself into the living room. The phone had rung several times, but she was unable to answer it. She had been on the floor about twenty-four hours.

Evelyn had not broken anything but was hungry and tired and hurting. We called her stepson and an ambulance. By the end of the week, she was in an assisted care facility. After about a week of physical therapy and regular meals, she was feeling much better.

I discovered through experiences like this that, even though I did not receive direct revelation, the Lord put me where He needed me to be.

—Elaine Stinnett

"I will go before your face. I will be on your right hand
and on your left, and my Spirit shall be in your hearts,
and mine angels round about you, to bear you up."

—Doctrine and Covenants 84:88

19

SHE LISTENED
WITHOUT JUDGING

One sister said that when her daughter was ten years old, the girl bravely came to her and her husband and told them she had been sexually molested. Feelings of devastation hit them in full force as one could only imagine. What made it even worse was when they learned it had been a member of their ward and a close friend.

She went to the bishop and the stake president, telling them of her heartbreak, her anger, and her desire not for revenge but justice. Both men's counsel was the same, "You need to forgive."

This sister was confused and hurt. She felt as if they hadn't listened. It seemed to her as if the offender was being shown more love than her daughter—the victim.

She walked with a friend in the mornings. One day, that friend asked her what was wrong, concerned over why she had not been acting like her usual happy self.

She started to cry and spilled out what had happened, openly discussing the situation, including her frustrations involving the recommendations she had received from the Church leaders. With discouragement and sadness, she wondered if she quit going to church, then maybe someone would understand her heart was overflowing with pain.

Her dear friend turned and said, "Stop that thinking now. Satan is telling you these lies. Pick up the Book of Mormon and read it. Get to know the Savior's love."

She did.

She read it from cover to cover for the first time. She learned about the Savior's suffering. She was not alone; He personally knew her pain. She learned to go to Him for the comfort and understanding she sought and eventually accepted the human weaknesses of her leaders.

That friend will forever have a special place in this sister's heart. She listened to her without judging and extended a hand of charity when she so badly needed it. Her daughter grew into a beautiful young woman with a strong testimony and counseling helped her deal with the scars of abuse.

She and her daughter have grown very close; she gained a greater knowledge of the Savior—something, she admitted, she might not have received any other way.

—Anonymous

"It is not for you to be led by the women of the world;
it is for you to lead the . . . women of the world, in
everything that is praiseworthy, everything that is God-
like, everything that is uplifting and . . . purifying to
the children of men."[18]

—Joseph F. Smith

20

MARY

*M*ary moved across country and into our ward, bringing with her four children, the heartache and bitterness of a nasty divorce from a husband who had lived a double life, and a deep questioning of the faith he'd baptized her into. Her siblings lived far away and didn't understand her "weird" religion, and her ex-husband's family, who did live close, was coping with their own challenges from the situation. Mary had moved away from everything familiar, relying on a Lord she wasn't sure she believed in anymore. She felt completely alone.

I was assigned as Mary's visiting teacher. For our first visit, my companion and I took Mary out to lunch. She shared some of her past struggles and bluntly told us of her doubts about the gospel. After that first visit, Mary couldn't believe the ward was so desperate they'd assigned a teenager to her (I look pretty young). She told the Relief Society president that she didn't want visiting teachers anymore, but, like an annoying housefly that won't leave, I didn't stop visiting. I could tell Mary needed a friend, whether she knew it or not.

Every couple of weeks, I would stop by with treats for her family and a sympathetic ear. Mary would talk for hours, and I just listened. I didn't judge her for her doubts and questions; I simply shared my conviction that the Lord loved her and she would be blessed if she stayed true to the gospel.

I tried to be aware of her family's needs. One time when I was grocery shopping, I thought I should get them some food too. I felt somewhat foolish when I showed up at their door with bags of groceries not knowing if they needed what I brought or would accept it as a gift. Months later, I found out that earlier that day, Mary and her children had been discussing whether or not people really cared.

Her son insisted that the ward members around them were good, but because Mary had been so wounded, she expected those who professed they cared would hurt her as soon as she let her guard down. When I had showed up out of the blue with bags of needed food, it seemed to be proof her son was right.

Mary slowly began to heal and trust people again. As caring home teachers and ward members helped her, her heart softened enough to begin letting the Lord back into her life.

One day, the school called Mary. Her seven-year-old had a terrible headache and was having trouble walking. Right away, the doctor sent him to the children's hospital for tests, where they discovered two brain tumors needing immediate surgery. Throughout the next three weeks of the resulting hospital stay, her son had five more surgeries and lost his vision.

The ward stepped in, and, with their support, Mary was able to stay at her son's side while he battled for his life. Relief Society sisters made sure the other children had somewhere to stay and rides to school and their activities. Others shuttled clothes and personal items back and forth from Mary's home to the hospital as needed. Some sisters helped with the bills and the upkeep of her house. Home teachers gave priesthood blessings, and the whole ward participated in fasts for Mary's family.

When Mary and her son came home, the service didn't stop. He had intense radiation treatments and a year of debilitating chemotherapy. Mary couldn't work, because he needed round-the-clock care. The sisters in the ward continued providing meals and rides as needed, sometimes giving respite care for an hour or two so Mary could have a break.

Through countless acts of good people following Christ's example, Mary saw that the Lord did love her and her children, and He hadn't left her alone.

Medical bills piled up, and I organized a neighborhood yard sale. Several ward sisters helped distribute flyers, gather donations, set things up, and run a bake sale. The donations poured in beyond our expectations. I had to recruit more sisters and several of their husbands to help—the yard sale became a ward project, taking up an entire cul-de-sac.

Over $6,000 was made for Mary's family. In between treatment, her son set up a table to sell Braille bookmarks. Friends from her home ward held a similar fund-raising event and raised another $4,000.

The year following her son's diagnosis, Mary faced other trials. She needed jaw surgery, broke her wrist, and dealt with innumerable challenges of a single mom raising children on her own, including a newly blind child undergoing cancer treatment.

Throughout it all, the sisters and brothers of our ward never stopped giving support. After the cancer treatment, Mary started training to become a nurse. The ward continued to rally around her during the years of school. Just recently, Mary graduated as a registered nurse.

Mary has grown steadily in the gospel because she saw and felt the Lord's love through others for so long. Her children gained testimonies of their own and strong ties to their ward family. The testimonies of the members in our ward grew through the unity we felt as we surrounded and supported Mary and her family.

That's how it's supposed to work; we uplift and help each other, so that we can return back to our heavenly home—together.

—Jaime Theler

If you can love each woman that you visit
because she is a mother of a home;

If you can find in each a lovely virtue—
then finding it—is sure to pass it on;
If you can disregard the littered parlor or dirty dishes that
you're sure to find;

but take your messages to the one who lives there
and make her feel you're friendly, wise and kind.

If you can sympathize where there is sorrow
calm the troubled waters where there's strife;

If you can make her know that her tomorrows
hold more than just the struggles of this life;

If you can help wherever help is needed,
share with her joys, as well as tears;

If you can leave a thought or inspiration
for her to carry with her through the years.

If she can confide in you when she's troubled,
and know that you, her confidence will keep;

If you can help a tired or weary mother
to make a bed or rock a child to sleep;

If you can do these things, and all the others
that I am sure are there for you to do,
yours is a mission not unlike the Master's
and blessings will be given unto you.

—Author unknown

21

CELEBRATE THEM!

She was new in our ward. Why on earth was she assigned to be my visiting teacher? We didn't get along. We were so different on the surface that it was hard to carry on a friendly conversation. It seemed as if we had come from different planets.

I loved being a mother—her kids made her crazy. My LDS roots were sure and deep—she was a convert who struggled with her testimony. I was intuitive—she was logical. Though we were both polite, we really got on each others' nerves.

Despite her struggling testimony and the tension between us, she kept coming. She rarely missed. Conversations were sometimes awkward. She came anyway. We disagreed often. She came anyway. Though our relationship was fragile, she found ways to serve me. She invited our family over for dinners and served us things we had never tried and things we couldn't afford. She offered to babysit and helped me with housework. She called to chat.

Gradually, a miracle began to happen.

We started to understand each other. She began to love me, and I couldn't help loving her back. We found that all of our differences were on the surface, and underneath we had much in common. We were more alike than we were different, and eventually we became dear friends.

Chieko Okazaki once said there is not one right way to be a Latter-day Saint woman, and she was right. Our strength can be found in our differences, not just our alikeness. If we were all intuitive, what would we do for logic? Our Father in Heaven made us different so that we could balance each other, strengthen each other, and learn from each other. Through my dear friend, I learned to appreciate differences. Now I celebrate them!

From a rough beginning grew a meaningful friendship, because my visiting teacher didn't give up. She kept coming. Though her testimony was fragile, she knew how to be a friend, and that is exactly what I needed.

Isn't that what everyone needs?

Though time and distance now separate us, we care deeply about each other. She is only a phone call away. Those phone calls are less frequent with each passing year, but they are just as meaningful. We are more than friends. We are sisters.

—Linda Garner

"When filled with God's love, we can do and see and understand things that we could not otherwise see or understand. Filled with his love, we can endure pain, quell fear. Forgive freely, avoid contention, renew strength, and bless and help others in ways surprising even to us."[19]

—John H. Groberg

22

WIPED OUT BY A SPROUT

It was a dank September afternoon in Southport, England, and I was in the early stages of pregnancy with our fourth child. As usual with my pregnancies, I felt so ill that all I wanted to do was curl up in a corner somewhere far away. Somewhere silent. And minus all smells.

Unfortunately, I was in the kitchen, preparing an evening meal, surrounded by three demanding little people, with no chance of curling up anywhere. Ever. Near or far.

I can still see the brussels sprouts. As I broke off each outer leaf, a powerful odor, which I don't normally notice, switched my stomach to overdrive. It was my breaking point. The long, sick day finally got to me, and those sprouts wiped me out.

The children had taken their noise into another room, and I collapsed into a chair by the table, dropping my head onto folded arms, weeping. I told Heavenly Father I was sorry I was such a hopeless mother, but I simply couldn't do this anymore. It was all so hard, and I was too sick to cope.

A few minutes later, the doorbell rang. I debated whether I had the strength to go and open the door, knowing that whoever was there would want to talk, and talking created saliva, which also made me throw up.

Somehow, I pushed through the "I can't do this" and did it. Was I ever glad! A dear LDS friend, who lived miles away, just happened to be passing my house and felt she needed to check up on me. She immediately took in the situation, suggested I went to bed for a while, and told me she would watch the children, finish preparing those nightmare sprouts, and make dinner.

What an angel! I've never forgotten Freda Whiteley's service to me that day, and the way she followed spiritual promptings that answered a prayer. Now, some thirty-four years later, I still think of her every time I peel a brussels sprout.

—Anne Bradshaw

"One kindness, one expression of love, one thoughtful gesture, one willing hand at a time . . ."[20]

— Kathleen Hughes

23

LEAP OF FAITH

Several years ago, we felt a strong prompting to move to the United States. Financially it didn't make sense—we were quite comfortable—but spiritually we knew it was the right thing. We only took clothes, some toys, and about three pieces of furniture.

Our first landing was in California. There ended up being challenges with the family we were staying with. It was a tough, emotional time. I quickly made friends with sisters in the new ward. They offered me emotional support and a shoulder to cry on—something I greatly needed.

It soon became apparent we couldn't stay in California, and we felt the Lord drawing us to Utah. Without a job or a house to live in, it made no sense, but we proceeded with faith. Angels from our ward gave us furniture, and we found a house to rent—the generosity and goodwill of these sisters was overwhelming. We left California with heavy but grateful hearts, hoping the Lord would see us through this leap of faith.

We discovered, after arriving in Utah, that the water pipes in the house we were to rent were cracked, had sprung a leak, and flooded the basement. We couldn't stay there until it was fixed. Discouragement hit hard, but before we left California, a dear friend had told us if we needed any help, to call her sister.

Feeling desperate, we did. She and her husband willingly opened their home to us while the problems at the rental house were fixed. What a blessing! We recognized the hand of the Lord in our lives as these angels were there to help us.

My husband got a job, but after a short while he became sick and was unable to go to work. The job was no longer available after he recovered enough to return. He began looking for something else.

The house we were renting went into foreclosure, and we had to move—we had no money. Christmas was coming, and we worried our children wouldn't have much for gifts. Then our cars were repossessed and we had no transportation.

It was a devastating time. The only thing we could think of to do was fall to our knees and plead with Heavenly Father for help. Again, angels came to our aid. Santa did come—in the form of anonymous "elves"—we found a home to rent through a family in our ward, and the same family lent us their truck to drive for a short time. Our bishop offered me a job at his business. Blessings and miracles once again!

The sweetest miracle came through a dear brother who was struggling with terminal illness. He fixed an old car and gave it to our family as a gift. Words cannot describe how humbled and grateful we felt. All we could do was cry and nod our thanks.

My husband went back to work, but it soon became apparent his illness was not going away. Learning how to accept this new reality has been difficult, but with Heavenly Father's gentle guidance, we were able to come to terms with what this meant to our family, and knowing the truth of our situation has been liberating.

Our family has been humbled and blessed through these experiences. Even though it has been difficult, we have never felt alone or abandoned. In fact, the angels around us in the form of friends, sisters, and brothers are evidence that Heavenly Father is aware of us, answers our prayers, and loves us more than we can comprehend.

—Anonymous

"We are surrounded by those in need of our attention, our encouragement, our support, our comfort, our kindness. . . . We are the Lord's hands here upon the earth, with the mandate to serve and to lift His children. He is dependent upon each of us."[21]

—Thomas S. Monson

24

THEY FILLED OUR KITCHEN AND OUR HEARTS

While a "poor college student" at BYU—and a new member of the Church—I had angels of mercy make an impact on my heart. One of my roommates was in the same "We have no money to go home for Thanksgiving" boat as me.

The other four girls had headed off to their respective homes, and most of the apartment complex was empty. Pat and I figured we would have peanut butter sandwiches for our Thanksgiving dinner and try to make the most of it. Both of us were sadder than we would admit.

That night, there was a knock at our door. Upon opening the door, we saw a huge box . . . with food! We carried in our gift box with two frozen turkey dinners, some rolls, fruit juice, a pumpkin pie, some treats, and a whole lot of loving hope to fill our kitchen—and our hearts.

A note (rhyming and cute—no idea what it said anymore) was attached, signed "Anonymous." But we knew it was our visiting teachers, who lived close by in the Utah Valley.

I honestly don't remember anything else about that Thanksgiving holiday. But I'll never forget the feelings of opening the door to see that box of food. My roommate and I laughed, jumped up and down for joy, dragged that box in, and reveled in the sweetness of being cared about.

It was more than food for the body—it was food for our souls. And it taught me, as a young woman, how a visiting teacher can impact another woman in huge and long-lasting ways.

Those girls probably have no idea—to this day—how very much they helped lift the spirits of two lonely, homesick roomies. I'm sure they don't realize how much we enjoyed every bit of that food. But I imagine they are still quietly and lovingly tending the sisters they visit teach.

I'm still trying to live up to the example these two young students set for me that November when I was a new member of the Church!

—Vickey Pahnke Taylor

"God has given the women of this church a work to do in building his kingdom. Know that you are daughters of God. Walk in the sun with your heads high, knowing that you are loved and honored, that you are a part of his kingdom, and that there is for you a great work to be done which cannot be left to others."[22]

—Gordon B. Hinckley

25

LOVING SISTERS—ANGELS HERE ON EARTH

J have been blessed with so many wonderful sisters in my life, particularly after this past year as we've gone through the trial of losing our son, Jacob. I have such a testimony of the love of my sisters and the strengthening power of service and compassion.

Sisters prepared meals during the two weeks Jacob was in a coma. Another sister came to the hospital so my husband and I could sleep in shifts without having to leave him alone. Sisters cleaned my home, made a beautiful memory quilt, and planted flowers a week after his death. Sisters from our former ward delivered books and a beautiful picture of Jacob with Christ, commissioned by a local artist.

Another sister and her husband, who we did not know personally, came to our home with money to help with funeral expenses and shared their testimonies of the strength they've found since losing two of their children in an accident.

My oldest daughter was married one week after Jacob's funeral. Sisters in our ward provided all the food for the wedding, helped decorate the church, and did my daughter's hair. Others have come by monthly since Jacob's death, on his birthday, and on holidays.

I could go on and on with many more wonderful ways sweet, loving, and inspired sisters have lifted our family in this time of need. The Lord truly is able to have his love extend to us through loving sisters—angels here on earth. Through them, we've been uplifted and have received answers to our prayers during a time when we weren't sure anything could help us heal or feel joy again.

—Cher Park

"Sisters, we are all in this together. We need each other. . . . Those of us who are old need you who are young. And, hopefully, you who are young need some of us who are old. It is a sociological fact that women need women. We need deep and satisfying and loyal friendships with each other. These friendships are a necessary source of sustenance. We need to renew our faith every day. We need to lock arms and help build the kingdom so that it will roll forth and fill the whole earth."[23]

—Marjorie Pay Hinckley

26

THE SERVICE OF FRIENDSHIP

I have a new friend, and she looks like chocolate," I told my parents when I came home on the first day of second grade. We had recently moved to the suburb of Maadi, just outside of Cairo, Egypt.

I was a Utah girl and, in 1978, had not known anyone who was a skin-shade darker than olive. When I met Abby, I was fascinated by the color of her skin. But at the age of seven, I didn't have a frame of reference to describe her, except for maybe chocolate-colored skin.

Abby and I became fast friends. We were both precocious girls who loved to play together at recess and sit together during class. Over the course of our friendship, we told many secrets to each other, passed notes in class, and even slept over at each others' homes. When we both moved back to the States, we shared sporadic letters while I was living in Utah and she in Chicago. Eventually we lost contact, but I'll never forget her as my first friend who didn't share the same religion, culture, or skin color.

I've often wondered how exactly a friendship starts and what draws friends together. Why do we immediately "click" with some and not with others? Most of my friendships have been slow transitions. It usually takes me quite a while to develop a trusting and strong relationship with another individual. But with

Abby, it seemed that our hearts were connected right from the beginning.

True friendship can be an incredible blessing in our lives. When I started writing my first book, I told no one except my husband. I was afraid to share it with even my closest friends. When I started opening up a couple of years later, I found the support overwhelming. I also joined a network of other LDS writers, which led to new acquaintances. I held back my friendship for the most part because I felt that I had a full life, plenty of relationships to keep track of, and friendships take time to cultivate and grow. Who had the time for one more?

I was sorely mistaken. In the past few years, I've met wonderful people who have become some of my dearest of friends. As we set aside the busyness of life and listen to promptings, we'll find that there is always room for one more person, just as the Savior makes room for each of us.

Friendship is a two-way street, and many times we are at the receiving end, but it's important to be at the giving end as well. As we extend our friendship to others, offering care and a compassionate ear, we are truly serving in the highest court possible. Many times in my life, an act of service has been the beginning of a good friendship. The example Christ set for us was not only to serve each other but to love each other, and that comes through cultivating friendships.

Marjorie Pay Hinckley said, "We need to renew our faith every day. We need to lock arms and help build the kingdom so that it will roll forth and fill the whole earth." I think of Sariah, wife of Lehi, and her life-changing journey into the wilderness. A camel caravan typically took about four months to travel the distance from the coast of Oman to the city of Jerusalem. Sariah's family spent eight years traveling that same distance. She was faced with many hardships, including giving birth in primitive conditions, trying to keep her family together, foraging for her growing family in a desolate terrain, and being asked by the Lord to no longer light fires, cutting off her ability to cook meat. How did Sariah cope with her burdens?

I believe she had a friend, perhaps many friends—certainly in her husband and in most of her children, but she also had Ishmael's wife. It comforts me to imagine that these two women shared their heartaches as well as their joys together, and that their friendship helped strengthen each other as they met their trials with faith and served each other in love.

—Heather B. Moore

"Some of the sweetness of sisterhood enjoyed by a worthy woman is the strength and love that comes through close association with other women in shared gospel pursuits. Sisters imbued with the spirit of the Lord have the desire to help others succeed and evidence a kind of selflessness that creates trust and lasting bonds of friendship."[24]

—Barbara B. Smith

27

SHARING THE GOSPEL

Don't you dare step into that Mormon church. You will go to [bleep]!" Cassia's mother had said this more than once. The sentence didn't need to be finished for my good friend, Cassia. She was Catholic, and I was Mormon. Yet we'd become the best of neighbors in a small apartment community in sunny Southern California.

Religion wasn't our only difference. She was Mexican; I was Caucasian. She was short; I was tall. She was outgoing; I was reserved. We were opposites in many ways, yet our spirits connected.

Our two boys were close in age and played together in the endless warm weather. Then we each had daughters. We swapped babysitting, organized playdates, talked about books and movies, and traded sewing techniques. But the question hung heavy in my mind—should I talk to her about my religion?

We'd had a few casual conversations, but nothing serious or "testimony" worthy. I didn't make friends easily, so I truly valued her friendship and didn't want anything to mar it. Yet I knew that if the roles were reversed, she wouldn't hesitate to share her testimony with me.

As a member of the Relief Society presidency in my ward, I had an upcoming Sunday lesson to teach. The topic was on friendship. Of course I thought of her a lot as I researched and prepared for the lesson. She had taught me many values in friendship, and I felt I'd learned as much from her as from any of my Mormon friends. But since her mother had been so vocal about the LDS church, I was hesitant. I didn't want to drive a wedge between them or make her choose on my account. After praying and deciding that the only thing I could do was ask, I invited Cassia to my lesson. I explained that it was a lesson on friendship—which made it a perfect lesson for her to attend.

Cassia's mother wasn't happy. She warned her, but Cassia decided to ignore her. Was it defiance of her mother, or curiosity, or both? When Sunday morning arrived, I was nervous. Cassia was coming to hear my lesson. I saw everything and everyone at church with new eyes—looking at them with a fresh perspective—wondering what it would be like to be attending for the first time.

My lesson went well even though I was a ball of anxiety. At the end, Cassia said she enjoyed it. Relief flooded through me. My prayers had been answered. Best of all, and much to her mother's surprise, Cassia came back in one piece, proving to her mother that she'd survived a Mormon church meeting.

Cassia started to attend a few "homemaking" nights with me and became friends with other LDS women. She made friends easily; it was just her nature. She was a genuinely compassionate and giving woman. I envied her at times when she could so naturally make friends and express herself. Often, I wondered if our roles had been reversed and I was really the Catholic friend to this naturally LDS woman.

By Halloween, Cassia's mother's heart had softened and she decided that our friendship didn't have any ulterior motives on my part. Cassia and her family, along with her mother, came to the ward Halloween activity. I gave her mother a tour of the beautiful stake center. She was impressed with the artwork that adorned the walls and the simple yet graceful appearance of the building.

As Christmas approached, I knew what gift I wanted to give to Cassia. I wanted to give her a Book of Mormon and share my testimony. But the doubts crept back in, and I didn't know if I had the courage to go through with it. I was afraid that it would put pressure on the friendship, or that she'd see it as an ulterior motive and our friendship would slowly dissolve.

Finally, unable to put off the promptings any longer, I wrote her a two-page letter, sharing my testimony and my gratitude for our friendship. I put the letter inside a Book of Mormon I'd purchased for her family. Then I prayed that she would know the pure intent of my heart and that she'd understand she wasn't on my to-do list to share the gospel with.

Christmas morning passed by in a rush, but my heart pounded whenever the phone rang. Was it Cassia? What did she think? Finally she called. With tears, she thanked me for the gift. She knew how important it was to me, and because I shared it with her, she knew how important she was. All of the worry and hesitation left me, and I knew that by following the prompting I'd been given, I'd become what she'd been to me all along: a true friend.

—Heather B. Moore

"As we go about our daily lives, we discover countless opportunities to follow the example of the Savior. When our hearts are in tune with His teachings, we discover the unmistakable nearness of His divine help. It is almost as though we are on the Lord's errand; and we then discover that, when we are on the Lord's errand, we are entitled to the Lord's help."[25]

—Thomas S. Monson

28

KATIE AND JULIE

When I was single, I was asked to be the Young Women's president in a ward considered to be in the "inner city" of Salt Lake City. For the first time in my life I wanted to say no. However, I accepted it as a call from the Lord and went to work.

There were ten young women in the program, some without the foundation of loving and stable homes. Their needs were especially great, and I found myself providing types of support I hadn't expected. Two girls in particular, Katie and Julie (names have been changed), came from one of the most difficult situations I had ever encountered.

I first learned about them secondhand from members who had spent extensive time in the ward and had tried, unsuccessfully, to set the family on a more secure path. Their voices were filled with discouragement. They felt that, no matter how hard they tried, it hadn't made a difference,

Katie and Julie lived in a crowded, dirty home that housed both their immediate and extended family members and multiple pets. The emotional climate was rocky, and they were often left to fend for themselves in negotiating the challenges of their teenage lives. They struggled in school and were ostracized by their peers. State welfare provided some income, but they didn't have the necessities of life and certainly no luxuries.

I don't remember my first impression of the girls, but I'm sure it included feeling overwhelmed by the task at hand. How do you support girls who have so many physical needs that it seems almost impossible to devote time to their spiritual needs? How do you get girls to come to church when no one else in their family does and other girls in the ward make fun of them? How was I supposed to help them?

I had to rely on the Spirit and instinct to extend myself and truly serve them.

I started gently encouraging them to wake up in time for Sunday meetings. Later I talked them in to coming to activities when they didn't want to. When Katie needed a place to get away from the angry yelling at home, she came to my apartment. When she needed to vent instead of participate in a mutual activity, I listened.

I gave Julie hugs and told her I was glad to see her. For our stake's Pioneer trek, I asked my mom to sew skirts for her so she could participate. I gave them rides to the activities not held at the church and hand-me-down clothes I no longer needed. I stood up for them and the support they needed from my presidency, even when it was difficult.

I love Katie and Julie, but those feelings didn't come by my own actions. They didn't come because of the things I did. The love came because God, that same God whose daughters they are, blessed me to feel that way. He opened a place in my heart for two girls who needed to feel His love. He led me to them at a point in my life when I had the time and resources with which to serve them. He blessed me to see their needs and empathize with them even though I had never walked in their shoes.

The things I was able to do did not change their lives completely. They still live in poverty and difficulty of all kinds. They still struggle spiritually. But Katie and Julie have come more than once as the years have passed to share their personal triumphs, however small, with me. They've addressed requests for help with the words, "I know you are someone who will help me." I share my love with them and encourage them to do their best.

Serving as a Young Women's president was a humbling experience. I feel greatly blessed to have forged a connection with those special young women and know I made a difference by serving in the Lord's vineyard.

—Cynthia Robbins Newman

"Love is what inspired our Heavenly Father to create our spirits; it is what led our Savior to the Garden of Gethsemane to make Himself a ransom for our sins. Love is the grand motive of the plan of salvation; it is the source of happiness, the ever-renewing spring of healing, the precious fountain of hope. As we extend our hands and hearts toward others in Christlike love, something wonderful happens to us. Our own spirits become healed, more refined, and stronger. We become happier, more peaceful, and more receptive to the whisperings of the Holy Spirit."[26]

—Dieter F. Uchtdorf

29

LAUGHTER AND LAUNDRY

*I*n 2001, we learned that our family was about to grow by
not one but two. We already had two daughters, one five
years old and one almost three. My pregnancy went well. I had
a few complications but was fortunate not to be put on bed rest
or hospitalized.

My mother-in-law was excited about the upcoming birth of
our twins. She went with me to the ultrasound to find out what
the babies genders were. She was hoping for two boys, at least one
for sure. We were having a boy and girl.

It was the middle of December, a cold Alaskan morning,
when they arrived via C-section, four weeks early. Our son had
trouble breathing but quickly recovered. Our daughter had club-
feet, and at less than a day old she was put in her first set of casts.

That night, our oldest daughter was in her first play at school.
It was also the night of our ward Christmas party. My husband
and mother-in-law went to the play, and a kind sister skipped the
ward party and came to the hospital to be with me. She also had
dinner ready when we came home from the hospital.

A few days later, our tiny daughter had her first appointment
for new casts. I wasn't able to drive yet, and another sister in the
ward had told me to call anytime if I needed help. I called and
asked her if she could take us to appointment. She willingly gave
up two hours of her day.

Keeping up with two young girls and two new babies was a big adjustment, and healing from the C-section complicated things more. That first month, life was one big blur. Being very independent, I struggled admitting I needed help, but I was blessed repeatedly with sisters that saw the need and stepped in.

One of my wonderful visiting teachers came often to hold one of the babies while I took care of the other one or got a few things done. Several times, my little son soaked his outfit while she was changing him. She laughed and cheerfully put him in another set of clean clothes. I was grateful she was there.

One of my biggest blessings was my wonderful mother-in-law. One day a week for several months, she drove over an hour each way, often on snowy and icy roads, to help me. She cleaned my house, frequently brought homemade bread and cookies, and washed loads and loads of laundry. I never appreciated clean, folded clothes, and fresh-smelling towels and sheets so much.

—Yvette Scott

"The Lord's love is often delivered through others as they respond to promptings of the Spirit. Are we hearing and following those promptings? . . . I fear sometimes we see the Lord's love only in the big events of our lives; we must also see His love in the smallest of things. Don't underestimate your ability to share His love through a simple, genuine gesture."[27]

—Bonnie D. Parkin

30

HIS TOOLS

I was a moody child. I had a hard time getting my math done, keeping things neat, and staying focused. When I was in a group of people, I couldn't stop talking, and yet my primary goal was to live in the mountains where I wouldn't have to be around anyone at all. I obsessed about the Holocaust and anything morbid, and planned out in detail what I would do if a holocaust came to our neck of the woods.

My personality stirred derision in my peers, but I know the Lord was aware of me. I always had one good friend—and she was never just like me. She was talented, outgoing, social, and cheerful, a girl with a lot going on who was put in my path to look past my quirks and my angst and love me for who I was.

By the age of thirty-five, I could see that I wasn't just moody; I was seriously depressed and had been since childhood. I spent hours, days, years, just looking out of windows while my mind whirred a mixture of images, conversation fragments, and memories over and over in a meaningless mess I call "blender brain."

I had a complicated marriage and three kids—one autistic. Sometimes I sat in front of the bathroom heater with the door locked while my son, the oldest, did his homework on the other side. That way, I could help without hurting him if he got an answer wrong.

It became obvious the problem wasn't going away, even when I jumped through the hoops of reading scriptures, saying prayers, and exercising—the touted cure for all slumps. I prayed in earnest to find a way to get over my mental health problems. I turned to a psychiatrist and tried a range of medications and a range of counselors. I grew noticeably worse.

The years passed.

I did my best with child-rearing and the callings I held in the Church. I was beyond discouraged and very frustrated that I wasn't accomplishing my goals. Inside, I was barely holding on. Through it all, I still, always, had at least one good friend—a friend who listened while I struggled to work through issues much bigger than my self.

I came to understand even more clearly that was how the Lord was blessing me. He was listening, and he hadn't left me alone. I began specifically praying to be led to people who could help me.

One sister mentioned something about hormones, and I felt the Spirit prompt me to try what she said. Another mentioned craniosacral therapy for autism. I took my daughter, and the therapist asked about me as well. That kind of therapy became a turning point for me. From others, I gleaned tidbits of information about wide ranges of medical practices and perspectives, and when the Spirit nudged me, I tried them. A conversation and the Spirit led to my diagnosis of bipolar disorder and a different kind of doctor.

No single person had all the answers to my specific problems, but I learned to let the Lord guide me, and He did—to many people who had no idea they were his tools.

—Jane Davis

"Our eternal happiness will be in proportion to the way that we devote ourselves to helping others."[28]

—George Albert Smith

31

LISTEN

One of my responsibilities as first counselor in the Relief Society presidency was to assist the teachers. At that time, we were blessed to have three spiritual, always prepared, and faithful teachers. That part of my job was easy. However, as often happens, one of our teachers was released and called to another auxiliary within the ward. Our new teacher was Rebecca.

We all knew Rebecca as a lovely and confident young mother with three preschool-aged children. Rebecca's love for life and her testimony of the gospel were evident by her ever-positive outlook and glowing countenance.

When it was time for her first lesson, I could tell she was extremely nervous. Over the next few lessons she taught, she barely glanced up at all as she read from the manual. It was awkward and uncomfortable.

As a Relief Society presidency, we prayed she would soon feel more at ease with her new calling. It was my responsibility, specifically, to help her. I had all kinds of ideas of what I was going to say to help Rebecca improve her teaching skills. After all, I was at least twenty years older, with years and years of experience teaching the gospel, right?

Feeling prepared, I went to the phone to call her. Before I completed dialing the number, I felt a prompting to stop, and I put the phone down. I had forgotten to pray. I did and received an answer—listen. It was that simple. Listen. Listen to Rebecca, and listen for the promptings of the Holy Ghost for guidance of what I should say to her.

Once we were on the phone, I asked Rebecca how she was feeling about her lessons. She started to cry. She explained how young, inadequate, and unqualified she felt to be teaching women more experienced in life and the gospel than her. She was ready to quit.

"What can they ever learn from me?" she sobbed.

She poured out her concerns, and I listened. "You're right," I said gently. "They do have more years of experience than you do—in life and the gospel. You can't change that, but I know you were called to this position for a reason."

We talked about different methods of teaching and ways she could draw upon the years of gospel knowledge and experience of the women. When we hung up, I could tell she was more relaxed and confident about teaching Relief Society. Rebecca went on to become one of our best teachers. The women responded to her humble desire to teach the gospel and fulfill her calling.

Several months later, she was giving a lesson on repentance and forgiveness. I was following along in the manual. She paused to explain a certain principle in her own words. Unexpectedly, tears sprang to my eyes. Rebecca put into words the answer to a concept regarding repentance and forgiveness I had been struggling with for years. The Holy Ghost confirmed it was the answer I had been seeking. What I learned that day in Relief Society has made a difference in my life.

I am thankful for the promptings of the Holy Ghost that guided me to know what to say to Rebecca, and that same spirit that guided Rebecca as she taught her Relief Society lessons.

—Pam Bolla

Because she is my sister
I will learn to really care
and to act with true compassion
for it is a privilege rare.
To extend my help and sympathy,
share her glad and dry her tears
and make her life more meaningful
by allaying many doubts and fears.

Because she is my sister
I will pray for special tools
that are not made in factories
and do not come from worldly schools.
I'll use my talents in her behalf,
my strength I'll add to hers
to make our testimonies grow
as the Gospel light within us stirs.

She's always been my sister,
even prior to mortal birth;
we just have different parents
for our sojourn here on earth.
I am my sister's keeper,
have always been since time began,
and I pray our association
will continue in the eternal plan.[29]

—Mary Clough

32

HE SENT ME ROSANN

*F*ive years ago, my son died unexpectedly. The outpouring of meals, cards, flowers, and well-wishers was overwhelming and much appreciated. Most of the people giving of themselves were neighbors, acquaintances, coworkers, friends, and family. A few weeks later it stopped. This was to be expected, but it was a painfully difficult time nonetheless.

During the day while my husband was at work and our other children were in school, it was especially hard and lonely. One dreary day in particular, I was feeling down, more than usual. I had been going through my son's things—holding his blankets, inhaling the scent of his clothing, and feeling sad that I had no one to talk to. In my boredom, I made the mistake of trying to pay some bills. With the funeral expenses, hospital bills, and loss of work, there wasn't enough money left.

I gave up trying to deal with the real world and threw myself on the couch, curled up into a ball, and sobbed—yet again. My emotional outburst was in full swing when I heard a soft knock at the door.

Oh great. Just what I need, I thought. *Someone to pity me while I try to keep composed.*

I heaved myself up off the couch and trudged over to the door, took a deep breath and opened it. Standing before me was a heaven-sent angel with fire-red hair; the concerned look on her face was one of pure sorrow. Rosann was a dear friend, former colleague, and sister in Zion.

I invited her in.

She listened while I spoke freely of my son. I showed her some of his special things. I cried openly—she wept with me. After our much-needed time together, she told me she had something for me. She pulled out a packet of cards, notes, and money collected from the faculty and staff of the school where I had previously taught. Words failed me as I read their expressions of kindness, realizing how great their sacrifice had been to help me and my family. Their donations, along with the generous help of my current school colleagues, would get us through our rough patch, financially.

I was overwhelmed with feelings of gratitude to the Lord. His divine intervention occurred that day and He sent me Rosann, my angel sister, when I needed her most—to pull me up when I couldn't do it myself.

—Amy Maddocks

"If I can stop one heart from breaking, I shall not live in vain.
If I can ease one life the aching, Or cool one pain,
Or help one fainting robin, Unto his nest again,
I shall not live in vain." [30]

—Emily Dickinson

33

INSTRUMENTS IN HIS HANDS

*I*t was a drizzly, cool morning the Tuesday before Thanksgiving. Driving to work, I was glad to be going in for the last day before a much-needed holiday break. My spirits were high as I anticipated the many activities planned with my immediate and extended family. I was overwhelmed with gratitude as I considered my many blessings and was reminded of the Lord's "tender mercies."

For some reason, I took a different route and at the last minute drove past my office to a nearby convenience store. Smiling and shaking my head at my sudden impulsiveness, I pulled into a parking space and decided to grab a quick drink. I shivered as I headed toward the entrance. Out of the corner of my eye, I noticed a young woman standing under the meager overhang, obviously trying to stay out of the weather. I wondered about her casually, thinking she probably was waiting for someone inside.

Heading back to my car a few minutes later, I noticed the young woman was now sitting on the concrete several feet from the door. She looked a little lost. She was dressed fairly well for the weather, but it was cold outside. I hesitated a moment, then surprised myself by walking toward her.

"Honey, are you okay? Do you need some help?" *What am I doing?* I thought. *You do not know who she is or if she's dangerous—and you're alone. No one even knows where you are.* I grinned nervously.

She told me she needed a ride to an apartment complex located a few miles away. She sprained her foot walking to a friend's house the evening before and ended up staying the night. That morning, her friend's mother left for work earlier than expected, and this woman wasn't able to get a ride home. She had tried walking a few blocks, but her foot ached with every step. When it started raining, she sought shelter in front of the store.

"Are you by chance going that way?" she asked.

I smiled. "I'm not, but I'd be glad to give you a ride if you're comfortable coming with me."

She nodded her thanks and hobbled over.

I'm trying really hard to follow thy promptings, Heavenly Father, I silently prayed, *and I know I was led here—please, please keep me safe.* As we drove out of the parking lot, I tried to start a conversation. I determined she was probably more frightened than I was.

She was new in town, with no family in the area. She had recently gone through a divorce and had moved to Utah to start her life over, hearing it was a good place and that jobs were available. She just started working at a credit union and had been worrying she wouldn't be able to make it on time for her afternoon shift. She really needed the job and was hoping it would become permanent after the holidays. Distressed over the situation, she had called her father in Wyoming. He agreed to come get her but wouldn't be able to leave until he finished work late that afternoon. She was prepared to spend hours waiting for him.

As I drove, she continued to talk. Her family life as a child hadn't been great, but she was determined to make a better life. She mentioned she had run into some missionaries from the Mormon Church. Having fond memories of going to an LDS church with her grandmother a couple of times in her youth, she eagerly stopped the missionaries to talk. She admitted not remembering much about the Church and the teachings, just that going made her feel happy. Those missionaries helped her find a better apartment and she was meeting regularly with them.

I smiled, now understanding why I had felt that undeniable prompting to help. I pulled into her apartment complex. "I'm a member of the LDS Church, and I know you will find both answers and happiness through the messages the missionaries are teaching. Did you pray for help this morning?"

"Yes," she said softly.

I put my car into park and turned toward her. "I am that answer to your prayer. I drove to that store not really knowing why. When I saw you, you looked like you needed help. This wasn't a coincidence. I was sent to give you a ride. Never doubt that your Heavenly Father knows who you are and that he loves you. Please keep studying with the missionaries."

She thanked me, and we exchanged pleasantries as she got out of the car. I watched for a minute as she walked toward her building, and then I headed back toward my office.

Humbled, tears quickly sprang to my eyes. I had been hoping to help someone that day, and Heavenly Father had kindly provided a way for me to do that. Thankfully, I had not let my fears stop me from following the prompting of the Holy Ghost. Instead, I was blessed to be "an instrument" in the Lord's hands.

When we have the courage to follow the promptings of the Holy Ghost, even when we don't always immediately understand those promptings, we have the opportunity to bless the lives of others and strengthen our own testimonies in the process.

—Debra George Hunsaker

"God does notice us, and he watches over us. But it is usually through another person that he meets our needs. Therefore, it is vital that we serve each other."[31]

—Spencer W. Kimball

34

The Stuff We Save

ere are the piles. Stuff we save goes here, this box is for goodwill, and this bag is for garbage," I said with authority. It was January second, the last day of Christmas break for my two teenage daughters, and I had decided to sift through twenty-two years of Christmas decorations.

"It will be fun," I added. Ally rolled her eyes and Olivia flopped on the LoveSac. I knelt by the largest tote and began pulling out something tangled with red raffia. Olivia sat up and grabbed a felt Santa door hanger.

"This is definitely garbage!" she exclaimed triumphantly. She stuffed the Santa in the garbage bag and grabbed a stack of chunky wooden angels. Ally went to the decorations I had used this year and began loading them into the designated tote.

"Mom," she said, "what about these?" In her hand were two wicker plate holders. Each plate held and framed a nylon face that was adorned with silk poinsettias, plastic holly leaves, and tiny golden bells. Santa had homemade wire glasses perched on his large nylon nose, a felt hat, matted cotton balls for his hair and beard. Mrs. Claus was the same with a small stitched smile, a tiny nose between rosy cheeks, and a candy-striped hat.

"Garbage," shouted Olivia.

"Now wait a minute," I said. "I made those."

"Mom you've made most of the stuff that's now in the garbage. What's so special about these?" Ally clapped the two plates together. Dust hung in the air and my mind raced back eighteen years. The story spilled out.

"I guess I was pretty naïve when we moved into the trailer park," I started. "I had heard the stereotypes all of my life but had never experienced them. It wasn't long before those labels began seeping onto me.

"I was at a school district meeting at the elementary school your older sister, Erica, was going to, and the people from the area that lived in 'houses' said they didn't want the 'trailer park' in the school boundaries. I took Erica visiting teaching with me one day—to the 'houses.' At first, the woman was excited to have her come and play with her daughter, who was the same age. When I told her where I lived, the excitement melted from her face. It made me sad and lonely, but I decided to embrace my trailer park neighbors.

"I made many of these Christmas decorations for those neighbors. Most of them didn't give back. I didn't care. I took a carload of kids to school each day. I was the carpool—the majority of the parents worked. I was happy to help.

"Liz was my next-door neighbor. She taught me how to make the Santa plates.

"I spent a lot of time with her. Her trailer was always filled with cigarette smoke, and each time I went in I said a silent prayer it wouldn't bother me. Looking back, I only remember her laugh. We had fun.

"She and her husband, Dean, were great people. I learned a lot about service from them. When I was eight months pregnant with you," I pointed to Ally, "it was August, and my swamp cooler went out. Your dad was out on a job and wasn't due back until late that night. Liz and Dean had planned a trip to Wendover and were leaving at 3:00 p.m., when Dean got home from work. I was miserable. When Dean got home, Liz sent him over. He worked on my swamp cooler until he got it fixed. They left for Wendover at 8:45 p.m."

I sat back, gazing at the two treasures that Ally had now placed on the floor. "These faces remind me of what I learned living in that trailer park." I looked at my daughters. "Remember to look beyond stereotypes. Remember to look at those around you as Jesus did. Some of the world's true treasures are those things that are out of date, shabby, or not what we're used to."

I watched as, together, Olivia and Ally wrapped my treasures in tissue paper and placed them in the "stuff we save" box. I smiled.

—Anita Wahlstrom

DEAR READERS,

I hope you've enjoyed reading this book as much as I have enjoyed writing and compiling it. Each story has touched me, and the personal experiences of my own I've included have strengthened my love for the many sweet sisters who've blessed my life. If you have a story you would like to submit for a future volume of *A Sisterhood of Strength*, send it to me for consideration at dionyg@gmail.com.

Notes

1. Mary Ellen Smoot, "Rejoice, Daughters of Zion," *Ensign*, November 1999, http://www.lds.org/ensign/1999/11 /rejoice-daughters-of-zion?lang=eng.
2. David O. McKay, *Man May Know for Himself* (Salt Lake City: Deseret Book, 1969), 261.
3   Gordon B. Hinckley, *Teachings of Gordon B. Hinckley* (Salt Lake City: Deseret Book, 1997), 696.
4. Jeffrey R. Holland, "To Young Women," *Ensign*, November 2005, http://www.lds.org/general-conference/2005/10/ to-young-women?lang=eng
5. Lucy Mack Smith, Relief Society Minutes, March 24, 1842, Archives of The Church of Jesus Christ of Latter-day Saints, 18–19.
6. Peggy A. McFarland, *Becoming Women of Strength* (American Fork: Covenant Communications, 1994), 65.
7. Boyd K. Packer, "The Circle of Sisters," *Ensign*, November 1980, 109.
8. Adapted from Cora Hill Arnold, "Shall I Deem Her My Enemy?" *Relief Society Magazine*, August 1970, 595.
9. M. Russell Ballard, "Women of Righteousness," *Ensign*, April 2002, http://www.lds.org/ensign/2002/04/women-of -righteousness?lang=eng.
10. James E. Faust, "You are all Heaven Sent," *Ensign*, November 2002, 111–12.
11. Margaret D. Nadauld, "The Joy of Womanhood," *Ensign*,

November 2000, www.lds.org/general-conference/2000/10/the-joy-of-womanhood?lang=eng.

12. Chieko N. Okazaki, "Strength in the Savior," *Ensign*, November 1993, http://www.lds.org/ensign/1993/11/strength-in-the-savior?lang=eng.

13. Mary Ellen Smoot, "Come, Let Us Walk in the Light of the Lord," *Ensign*, November 1998, http://www.lds.org/ensign/1998/11/come-let-us-walk-in-the-light-of-the-lord?lang=eng.

14. Dieter F. Uchtdorf, "Lift Where You Stand," *Ensign*, November 2008, 56.

15. Karen Lynn Davidson, "Each Life That Touches Ours for Good," *Hymns of The Church of Jesus Christ of Latter-day Saints* (Salt Lake City: The Church of Jesus Christ of Latter-day Saints, 1985), no. 293.

16. Becki Madsen, "My Sister's Hands," n.d., http://defordmusic.com/mysistershands.htm.

17. M. Russell Ballard, "Women of Righteousness," *Ensign*, April 2002, 67–73.

18. Joseph F. Smith, *Teachings of Presidents of the Church: Joseph F. Smith*, (Salt Lake City: The Church of Jesus Christ of Latter-day Saints, 1998), 184.

19. John H. Groberg, "The Power of God's Love," *Ensign*, November 2004, 11.

20. Kathleen H. Hughes, "That We May All Sit Down in Heaven Together," *Ensign*, November 2005, http://www.lds.org/ensign/2005/11/that-we-may-all-sit-down-in-heaven-together?lang=eng.

21. Thomas S. Monson, "What Have I Done for Someone Today," *Ensign*, October 2009, 86.

22. Gordon B. Hinckley, "Live Up To Your Inheritance," *Ensign*, Oct. 1983, http://www.lds.org/general-conference/1983/10/live-up-to-your-inheritance?lang=eng.

23. Virginia H. Pearce, *Glimpses into the Life and Heart of Marjorie Hinckley* (Salt Lake City: Deseret Book, 1999), 254–55.

24. Barbara B. Smith, "The Bonds of Sisterhood," *Ensign*, March 1983, http://www.lds.org/ensign/1983/03/the-bonds -of-sisterhood?lang=eng

25. Thomas S. Monson, "Three Gates Only You Can Open," *New Era*, August 2008, 6.

26. Dieter F. Uchtdorf, "You Are My Hands," *Ensign*, May 2010, 70, 75.

27. Bonnie D. Parkin, "Eternally Encircled in His Love," *Ensign*, November 2006, 109–110.

28. George Albert Smith, as quoted in *Daughters in My Kingdom* (Salt Lake City: The Church of Jesus Christ of Latter-day Saints, 2011), 77.

29. Mary Clough, "Because She is My Sister," www.geocities.ws /perudol1/bdgift.htm.

30. Emily Dickinson, as quoted on http://www.wisdomquotes .com/quote/emily-dickinson-6.html.

31. Spencer W. Kimball, "The Abundant Life," *Ensign*, July 1978, www.lds.org/ensign/1978/07/the-abundant-life?lang=eng.

Contributing
PUBLISHED AUTHORS

Amy Maddocks—wife, mother, and educator—is the author of *Too Precious for Earth*, a book about the grief one experiences when losing a child. She is also a contributing author to *Angels Bear You Up*. Learn more about Amy on her website: www.amymaddocks.com.

Anne Bradshaw was born in Wales and raised in Cheshire, England. She is a wife and mother of four, a grandmother, and the author of several published books, including *True Miracles With Genealogy*, volumes 1 and 2, and *Famous Family Nights*. You can learn more about Anne at her website: www.annebradshaw.com.

Cheri Chesley, wife and mother of five, believes in miracles. She is the author of *The Peasant Queen* (a young adult novel), *The Wild Queen*, *The Tyrant King*, and the novella *The Ghost Bride*. Visit her website for more information: www.cheri-chesley.com.

Connie Sokol—wife and mother of seven, local and national presenter, and *Deseret News* columnist—is the author of five books. Her latest, *Motherhood Matters*, was released just in time for Mother's Day in 2012. You can visit her website, www.8basics.com, for more information about Connie and her books.

Deanne Blackhurst is a full-time writer, wife, mother of eight, and grandmother of three. She is the author of *Turning Hearts*, and *Sleight of Hand*, her third book—a suspense novel—will be released in 2013. Visit www.deanneblackhurst.com to learn more.

Haley Hatch Freeman is a wife, a mother of three, and an anorexia survivor. She is the author of *A Future for Tomorrow: Surviving Anorexia—My Spiritual Journey* and is a public speaker to youth and women's groups. Learn more about Haley and her inspiring work at www.haleyhfreeman.com.

Heather B. Moore is a wife, mother, and award-winning author of several historical novels set in ancient Arabia and Mesoamerica, author of one nonfiction book, and coauthor of *Christ's Gifts to Women*. She also manages the editing company Precision Editing. Learn more at www.hbmoore.com.

Jaime Theler is a wife and stay-at-home mom of three, is addicted to books and running, doesn't like chocolate, and is the author of *Enjoying the Journey: Steps to Finding Joy Now* and coauthor of *Parenting the Ephraim's Child*. Learn more on Jaime's website, www.jaimetheler.blogspot.com.

Jodi Robinson, wife and mother of four, is a speaker and the author of the inspirational book *Women of Virtue*. Her firesides and presentations inspire youth and women to believe in the power of virtue. You can visit Jodi's website to learn more: www.jodimarierobinson.blogspot.com.

Linda Kay Garner is a wife, mother of seven, grandmother of twenty-one, and author of *Some Secrets Hurt*—a picture book designed to prevent sexual abuse—and *His Grace is Sufficient: Finding Healing through Jesus Christ*. Linda is also the founder of the No More Secrets Foundation. You can learn more about Linda and her work at www.somesecretshurt.com.

Lori Nawyn is the wife of a fireman, a mother of four, and a grandmother of two. The author of *My Gift To You*, an inspirational novel, she's also a freelance artist and is the illustrator of the children's book *What Are You Thinking?* Visit Lori's website to learn more: www.lorinawyn.com.

Roslyn Reynolds is a single mom, a grandmother, a speaker, and the author of *Solo: Getting It All Together When You Find Yourself Alone*, a practical guide for those who are grieving, and the audio CD *Seven Steps to Healing and Hope*. Visit her website to learn more: www.roslynreynolds.com.

Vickey Pankhe Taylor is a wife, mother, grandmother, speaker, songwriter (whose music includes songs for the Especially For Youth program), and the author of *Apron Strings: Tender Ties Between Mothers and Daughters*. You can learn more about Vickey at her website, www.goodnessmatters.com.

About the
—❧· AUTHOR ·❧—

Diony George is a wife, stay-at-home mom of seven, grandmother of two, public speaker, and the author of three
books. A former Young Women president, ward Relief Society
president, and counselor in the stake Relief Society presidency,
she loves helping women draw closer to the Savior. She's an avid
reader, whose favorite genre is romantic suspense. Diony loves
to travel, sew, and bake—especially pies and homemade bread.
Born and raised in Alaska, she currently resides in Salt Lake City
with her husband and family.

Ms. George can be reached through her personal website at
www.dionygeorge.com.